The Successful

CFO

The key focus areas the CFO must master

Tony Tripodo

The Successful CFO; Key Focus Areas the Successful CFO Must Master is published under Mission books, sectionalized division under Di Angelo Publications INC.

MISSION BOOKS

an imprint of Di Angelo Publications The Successful CFO; Key Focus Areas the Successful CFO Must Master. Copyright 2017 Tony Tripodo in digital and print distribution in the United States of America.

Di Angelo Publications

4265 San Felipe #1100

Houston, Texas, 77027

www.diangelopublications.com

Library of congress cataloging-in-publications data

Tony Tripodo The Successful CFO; *Key Focus Areas the Successful CFO Must Master*. Downloadable via Kindle, iBooks and nook.

Library of Congress Registration

Hardback

ISBN-10: 1-942549-29-6

ISBN-13: 978-1-942549-29-1

Layout: Di Angelo Publications

Cover Design: Di Angelo Publications

Authors are available for speaking opportunities and engagement seminars, for information please contact Di Angelo Publications.

1. Non Fiction

2. Non Fiction—Finance & Business—United States of America with int. Distribution.

DI ANGELO PUBLICATIONS

A Modernized Publishing Firm

"Tony's long and distinguished career as a C suite executive affords him an unparalleled viewpoint on the characteristics of what it takes to become a successful CFO. Being named a CFO is not the culmination of a career in finance, but in many ways is the beginning of a journey to becoming a trusted partner to the CEO, executive management team and of course, the board of directors. Tony's leadership, strategic thinking and professional mentoring skills will be of great benefit to all that read his book. Embrace his wisdom, read with an open mind, accept responsibility for you and your team's actions and you too will be on your way to becoming a highly trusted business advisor."

Lloyd Hajdik
EVP and CFO
Oil States International

"In my 25+ year career in commercial banking I have never dealt with a CFO that brought a more balanced and thoughtful perspective to the role than Tony. He has always had a very insightful perspective that is refreshing and appreciated by the banking community that he has worked with over the years."

David A. Batson
Commercial Banker

"Tony is a thoughtful, talented CFO with an excellent understanding of the issues that drive the industry and his company. He takes a pragmatic approach to his role learned over many years of direct experience, and he is one of the more exceptional corporate officers that I have worked with in my 20+ years in banking...."

Scott Warrender
Managing Director
Wells Fargo Securities

"Tony Tripodo has fully experienced the ups and downs of the oil & gas industry over the past 40 years. Throughout this exciting and turbulent period, he has consistently demonstrated good cheer, a positive attitude and creative decisionmaking as CFO."

Osmar Abib
Global Head of Oil & Gas
Credit Suisse

Dedication

To my parents, Charles and Anna, the product of poor Italian immigrants who selflessly dedicated their entire life so that their children could enjoy a better life.

Epigraph

"One life stamps and influences another, which in turn stamps and influences another, on and on, until the soul of human experience breathes on in generations we'll never even meet."

Mary Kay Blakely

Prologue

The Successful CFO

Over the years, the influence of chief financial officers in the business world has expanded. Chief financial officers are expected to play a major role in not only guiding the financial affairs of their organizations, but also to assist the Chief Executive Officer and the executive management team with overall strategic planning. The chief financial officer is often viewed by boards of directors and outside stakeholders as the second most important executive in any organization.

The emergence of global competition from many new corners of the world is forcing CFOs to expand their perspective far beyond the borders of their home country. The Sarbanes-Oxley Act of 2002 enacted in the wake of well-known accounting scandals added a significant layer of complexity to the role of the CFO. The financial meltdown of 2008 has further served to highlight the critical role the CFO plays in the business world. Legislation that was passed by the federal government post-2008 has made the extension of credit by financial institutions more complicated and perhaps more difficult as well. All-in-all, CFOs have had to up their game.

Let me make it clear from the start by saying that this book is not about me. During my forty plus year career in the business world, mostly as a chief financial officer (CFO), but also as a board member, business owner and accountant, I have committed more than my fair share of mistakes. I don't hold myself up as the model CFO. Hopefully, though, I have learned from the mistakes I've made.

The Successful CFO

Over the course of these forty years, I have witnessed successful companies and companies that have failed as well. I have also observed individuals whom I considered to be very effective CFOs. Conversely, I have met some individuals that hold the title of CFO who struggled to make a difference for their companies.

My first promotion to the position of CFO came when I was in my mid-thirties. Years later, I would look back at the way I initially approached the job as CFO and say to myself that I wish I knew then what I know now. To say it another way, throughout my career as CFO, I would have greatly benefitted from reading a book like the one I have written here.

This book is about my collective experiences in learning what works and what doesn't work, thus motivating me to share these experiences with the hope that other chief financial officers or those individuals that aspire to be chief financial officers, as well as individuals responsible for overseeing the work of chief financial officers will benefit from my collective experiences.

I will have considered this book a success if the reader finds a few pearls of wisdom or can relate to shared experiences that inspire and influence the reader in a positive manner translating to making a more successful CFO. If you are not already a CFO, but aspire to be one, the book succeeds if it provides a better understanding of what it takes to become a more successful CFO.

I do like to quote people that I find particularly thoughtful and I liberally sprinkle quotations from these individuals throughout this book. Some of these quotations are from business people and while others are from individuals outside the business world. The quotes I have chosen are meaningful to me and I wish to share them in order to help illustrate and drive home the underlying message of my work.

"Don't be embarrassed by your failures. Learn from them and start again."[1]

---

1   Sir Richard Branson, founder of the Virgin Group

Table of Contents

Introduction

This book is more philosophical than prescriptive, more holistic than technical, focusing on the qualitative attributes necessary for a CFO to succeed. I do get mildly prescriptive when delving into the subject matter of cash flow forecasting (Chapter 4) and the generation of timely financial information (Chapter 5) but overall the book stays fairly qualitative in general. This book is more about approach, mindset and leadership.

How to optimize or calculate return on capital or return on equity; you won't find these subjects discussed in this book. Neither will you find me discussing debt versus equity ratios, working capital ratios, gearing ratios or the like. This book is not about technical financial metrics at all. The libraries of academic institutions and business schools are replete with books that teach and discuss these subjects.

Every company has a unique set of dynamics and challenges that compel the CFO to focus his or her attention in one area more than another. Publicly traded companies have the added dimension of requiring CFOs to contend with the capital markets. Non-profit organizations have their own unique set of characteristics and challenges that don't involve maximizing profits or capital returns. Private equity held companies often present the CFO with a completely different environment and expectations as owners of these companies are often motivated to return invested capital to their equity investors in a relatively expeditious time frame. Startups typically require the CFO to stay on the constant treadmill of raising capital for their company to meet its growth aspirations. Again, every company has differing strategic objectives and balance sheet profiles that need to be addressed by the chief financial officer. There is no one-size-fits-all financial strategy that can be applied to every company in the business or the not for profit world.

Although every company has a different set of characteristics and challenges, I believe there are some common success factors crucial for a CFO to accomplish which transcend company-specific profiles. I use the word 'company' to encompass all organization types, including not-for-profits. Admittedly, a lot of the subject matter of this book is geared toward CFOs of for profit entities. However, the CFO of a non-profit organization can and should benefit greatly from much of the material addressed in this book.

If the CFO is able to accomplish the success factors addressed in this book, I believe they should be well on their way of becoming a successful CFO.

These success factors are:

- Transitioning from Doer to Influencer

- Hiring and Developing Talent

- Translating Financial Information

- Managing the Balance Sheet

- Generating Timely Information

The first five chapters explore each one of these success factors. In my opinion, the first success factor enumerated above, "Transitioning from Doer to Influencer", may be the most important success factor for the CFO to accomplish. Mastering this success factor will make it so much easier for the CFO to achieve success on the other four factors. For instance, if the CFO builds the relationships needed and obtains an intimate understanding of his or her company's business, the ability of the CFO to influence needed changes to the company's credit policy becomes much easier to achieve (Chapter 4).

In the last chapter of this book I address three areas that the CFO should approach with a great deal of caution. While these are areas that the CFO might have in his or her job description, the CFO should be very careful about expending too much time and effort. I will explain why.

Chapter One

Transitioning From Doer to Influencer

The Successful CFO

Many CFOs started their careers as accountants, auditors, or bankers (commercial or investment). I have met CFOs that started out in the human resource function or were lawyers. Many CFOs possess advanced degrees such as a Master's in Business Administration (MBA) or Master's in Accounting. There is no one technical or academic background that produces a more successful CFO vis-à-vis another. Don't get me wrong, education and training are vital and serve as a cornerstone for any individual's ascent up the career ladder. However, it's how the CFO approaches the job that is the most important ingredient in becoming a successful CFO.

It seems as if many individuals I have met who were promoted to the position of CFO started their careers as accountants or auditors. Accountants and auditors possess the experience and education in their professional background which makes them proficient in financial statement literacy and financial metrics. Accountants and auditors are often well equipped to translate complex financial statement information to various stakeholders: management, employees, boards of directors, investors, financial analysts, etc. However, having an accounting or auditing background does not guarantee success as a CFO unless that individual can master the success factors discussed in this book. Don't for a minute think that just because you may not have an accounting or auditing background, that you can't be a successful CFO. Master the five success factors and you are in a great position to succeed.

The Successful CFO

I started my career as an auditor working for a Big Four accounting firm and ultimately moved into the tax discipline. Later on in my career I was hired on to become the Director of Taxes for a large multi-national energy company. My job performance was dependent upon sifting through complex cross border transactions in order to optimize (minimize) the tax impact to the company. Detailed technical memoranda were written documenting the support for my conclusions and often citing esoteric tax rulings. The work was highly technical and required a fair amount of "book" knowledge and research. There was plenty of **Doer** in order for me to successfully perform my professional responsibilities.

Several years into my tenure with this particular company, the head of Human Resources approached me suggesting I consider moving into a finance role working as the Controller of a major business unit. I accepted the opportunity seeing the potential for not only broadening my business perspective but also providing a wider path of career advancement opportunities versus strictly focusing in the highly technical corporate tax arena.

After a relatively short period of time, I was promoted from Controller to CFO of this particular business unit. I quickly realized that my fellow business unit executives could care less about my technical accounting and tax skills. What they really wanted to know was whether I was more than a run of the mill "bean counter"; someone who would work as an integral part of a team committed to adding meaningful value to the company through teamwork and knowledge of the business. Certainly, overseeing the finances of the business unit as well the accurate preparation of monthly, quarterly and annual financial information was an essential job responsibility. However, real value to the company went way beyond performing the work of a traditional accountant.

Adding meaningful value is not rocket science, but applying good old fashioned managerial and people skills. The most critical of these skills can be distilled down into two key areas:

- Building relationships with fellow members of your management team and key individuals throughout the company as well as with important external stakeholders.

- Developing an intimate knowledge of the business. A CFO cannot succeed unless he or she develops a keen sense of what is driving the business; i.e., what activities are behind the numbers. It is important for the CFO to learn what activities are working well for the company and conversely, what activities were not working well and why. The CFO must put himself or herself in a position where they can clearly articulate problem areas of the business and demonstrate to the CEO and the rest of the management team that they have a clear understanding and practical knowledge of what makes their company tick.

Relationship Building

"The business of business is relationships; the business of life is human connection."[2]

I don't pretend to be an expert on relationship building. There are many well regarded management gurus who have studied the subject, and a good many of whom have written thoughtful books and articles advising readers on the best way to build relationships. All I know and must emphasize is that relationship building is crucial for a CFO to succeed.

Building relationships throughout a company is critical, but the most important relationship the CFO must develop is with the lead executive of the company. Regardless of title, I will use the acronym, CEO, to describe the lead executive, whether that individual carries the title of Chief Executive Officer, President, Managing Director, Executive Director, or whatever. The relationship between the CEO and the CFO must develop to the point where the company perceives that there is very little separation between the two. Now, this doesn't mean that the CFO should become a "yes person." In fact, any CEO-CFO relationship should leave plenty of room for a healthy, respectful dialogue involving differences of opinion on strategy, tactical business decisions, balance sheet management, etc. Often times, the CEO and CFO have different views about where money should be spent and what investments their company is or should be making in order to build sustainable value. I believe a healthy relationship exists be-

---

2   Robin Sharma, author

tween the CEO and the CFO when their relationship has developed where they both expect differences of opinion on many business issues.

"It's lonely at the top" is an expression that is often expressed by and about the CEO. After all, it's the CEO who is ultimately responsible for the success or failure of the organization, the execution of strategy, the livelihood of those employed in the company, etc. When the CEO views the CFO as his or her trusted advisor, their consigliere, then the relationship between the two has probably been fully developed. To the extent that the CFO can make the CEO's life a little less lonely, the CFO is on the road to succeeding.

My experience and observations suggest that the CFOs that seemed to gain the most respect by the CEO, and for that matter the rest of the company, were the ones that challenged the thought process of their CEO to the point that the CEO would consider, from time-to-time, alternative paths to reaching a desired business objective or strategy, or in fact, perhaps not pursuing a particular business objective or strategy. The level of respect the CEO has for the CFO, which must be earned, will go a long ways to determining how influential the CFO becomes in his or her company. Master the five success factors discussed in this book and the CFO should earn that respect.

While the CEO-CFO relationship is critical to the effectiveness of the CFO, relationship building certainly does not stop there. The CFO needs to seek out key individuals throughout the company to build relationships. The more relationships that are built and nurtured, the more influence the CFO will have in any company and the more persuasive the CFO will be. Throughout my career, I have consistently found that the most critical relationships to develop were with people who occupied the following or similar executive level positions:

- Chief Operating Officer

- General Counsel

- VP- Human Resources

- Chief Manufacturing Officer.

I offered up the four above as it is likely that the CFO will interact with these individuals quite often. I listed these four with some hesitation as I don't want to suggest that relationship building stops with these functional heads. Again, I emphasize the importance of building relationships up and down the management ladder, from lower levels of the organization all the way to the top.

In addition, the CFO should make a special point of developing relationships with key accounting and finance personnel who do not reside at the head office. When I was a business unit CFO of a major company, we were constantly asked to produce reports and analysis for the head office, often times with scant explanation for why these reports were needed. We were just asked to do it! More often than not, these reports were ad hoc requests (and far from routine), so our accounting systems were not geared up to quickly and easily prepare the requested reports. The effort expended by my staff was time consuming and we often did not see the value of the exercise to our business unit nor did we understand how these reports were of value to the company as a whole. An unhealthy level of cynicism and resentment crept into the attitudes of the finance and accounting team over these corporate requests and it was difficult for me, as CFO, to tamp down the negative emotions. The cynical and negative emotions expressed by my staff simply resulted from the lack of relationship building by the head office. Rarely did key members of the corporate finance and accounting team visit our business unit. These individuals seemed to be content hanging out in the ivory tower. What a missed opportunity for the head office staff to build relationships and morale among the troops. The mere effort by the CFO of the head office in visiting business units and other operational facilities outside the head office and to interact with personnel at the operating level (and for that matter key corporate finance and accounting personnel) and putting "face to name" will facilitate the efficient generation of information flow from business units to corporate.

Again, every company has different characteristics and certainly relationships need to be developed beyond the C-suite. The most important point here is to *build relationships*.

Building relationships does not require you to hit the bar or the pub every night with your co-workers or play golf or tennis, or engage in other social activities. Judiciously, there is a time and place for socially oriented activities with co-workers. I certainly do believe that when the CFO visits his or her company's business locations outside of the locale of the home office, he or she should seek out opportunities to engage with local management in a more social setting as well as in the workplace. My experience is that most executives work hard, are exhausted at the end of the day and prefer to spend their evenings at home or their weekends on family activities. The most important and valuable relationship building occurs at the office between 8 a.m. and 6 p.m., so to speak. The CFO does not need to become best buddies with his or her fellow co-workers in order to establish meaningful working relationships in the company.

Developing an Intimate Knowledge of Your Business

"To succeed in business, to reach the top, an individual must know all it is possible to know about that business"[3]

Building relationships is merely the beginning of becoming an *Influencer*. It's not enough to build relationships without adding an intimate knowledge of the business to the CFO's toolbox.

Let me define the term "intimate knowledge of the business" by defining what it doesn't mean as it applies to the role of the CFO. Let me begin with some exaggerated examples:

---

3   J. Paul Getty, founder of the Getty Oil Company

The Successful CFO

The CFO of the National Football League (NFL) doesn't need to be able to get on the football field and duke it out with three hundred pound athletes or be able to throw a football sixty yards downfield. It might help if the CFO had once played the game in his youth, but even that's not necessary to function in the role. It doesn't mean that the CFO of Southwest Airlines needs to get her pilot's license and learn how to fly a Boeing 737. It doesn't require that the CFO of Chevron to be able to operate the drilling rigs that her company employs to explore for oil and gas.

At a more mundane level, it doesn't require the CFO to skillfully operate the CNC (Computer Numeric Control) machines on the manufacturing floor of the factory which makes the company's products.

Most CFOs have accounting, finance, business or law degrees. It would be very difficult for CFOs to start from scratch, and learn how to engineer the products his or her company manufactures, and they probably wouldn't be very good at it. CFOs are trained as accountants, financiers, or lawyers because as they probably learned early on, they had a native ability that revealed itself in their formative years that allowed them to learn those disciplines and learn those disciplines well.

It's not enough for the CFO to be known as a good guy or gal. In order for the CFO to earn the credibility necessary to positively influence the management team requires the CFO to understand the business of his or her company in quite some depth. This often takes time and effort and again, every company is different—both in terms of complexity and footprint. However, there are some bits of advice I can offer to help a CFO learn the business.

First and foremost, get up from behind your desk and leave your office!!

So where should the CFO go?

- If your company is in the manufacturing business, walk the manufacturing floor. See how your company builds the product it sells. Observe how your company's products get converted or assembled from raw materials to end product. Speak to the machinist, the warehouse clerk, the factory superintendent. Listen to their gripes, I guarantee you they will have some. Speak to the employees who are involved in the supply chain and genuinely listen to the challenges they face in facilitating the flow of goods and services required to manufacture the company's products. Take your observations back to the office and see if you can translate these observations into a better understanding of the activities that went into the actual product cost that is reflected in your financial systems.

- If your company has district or regional sales offices, take the time to travel and visit these locations. The rest of the company will take note of your visits and respect your willingness to learn something about the business.

Make your visits meaningful; spend your time listening and observing. Certainly, you will learn some aspects of the business closer to the customer interface. When the CFO returns to the home office they will be in a much better positon to influence change.

- Visit customers. Occasionally, ask to accompany the sales force or marketing personnel when they make a "sales call." The CFO will develop a better understanding of why your customers buy your product or use your services and how the company could possibly add value for their customers. You will better understand the competitive advantage your company's products or services provide your customers. Conversely, you may learn where your company's product or services fall short.

- Attend operational meetings. Listen to the challenges that operating personnel have in order for the company to achieve a high level of customer or client satisfaction. A better understanding of these challenges could alter the CFO's views on how the company can best invest limited financial resources.

Again, spend as much or more time out of your office as opposed to sitting behind your desk. Spend more time listening than talking. This is common sense advice; individuals learn more by listening than talking. A good listener is also better at building relationships than individuals who like to (hear themselves) talk.

The Successful CFO

The objective of these efforts is to gain an intimate understanding of the business which will allow the numbers you review in financial reports to "come alive." When gross margins decline by two percentage points, the CFO should have the intimate business knowledge of why this occurred. See Chapter Three – Translating Financial Information.

Most sales and marketing personnel I have worked with have impressed me as having a deep knowledge of the products and services they sell. Many of these sales and marketing personnel have engineering or technical backgrounds—a distinct advantage. Others that didn't, took it upon themselves to obtain a deep and thorough knowledge of the products and services offered by their companies. In a highly competitive business, it is imperative that sales and marketing personnel have the ability to articulate the advantages of the products and services they sell with the knowledge to compare and contrast from the competition. Although the CFO does not have to develop anywhere near as deep a knowledge as the salesforce, it is important for the CFO to learn enough about how his or her company's products or services are of value to the end consumer to be able to articulate what the company does for a living to various constituents: investors, boards of directors, etc. If the CFO makes an effort to learn, the executive management team will respect his or her willingness to grasp the fundamentals of how their company's products function or how its services are delivered.

If the CFO's company offers fundamental training courses on the products and services sold, the CFO should take advantage and attend these courses.

In addition to developing an intimate knowledge of the business, the CFO needs to gain a good understanding of the competitive landscape in their company's industry. At a minimum, investors will expect the CFO to articulately explain the company's position versus the competition. I can't tell you how many times I have been asked an "out of the blue" question by an investor based on something the investor was told by a competitor on how some new widget the competition developed was going to take over the world and put us out of business. The more you are prepared to answer these questions, the better the CFO will do at representing the company.

Building key relationships and gaining first hand, intimate knowledge of your company's business are the two ingredients that when added to your technical (academic) skills, transform the CFO from a **Doer** to **Influencer**—and likely a **Positive Influencer**.

The success factor, **transitioning from Doer to Influencer**, permeates and facilitates every aspect of the CFO's job performance and is the primary skillset that will allow the CFO to succeed with the other four success factors discussed in this book.

Chapter Two

Hiring and Developing Talent

The Successful CFO

"The best executive is one who has sense enough to pick good people to do what he wants done, and self-restraint enough to keep from meddling with them while they do it."[4]

I will start this chapter with a real life experience that drove home the importance of surrounding yourself with talented, motivated individuals.

As parents, we are often called upon to volunteer to coach our children's youth sports teams. When my youngest son was in second grade, the athletic department of his school solicited parents to volunteer to coach the boys' soccer team. So wanting to be a good citizen along with a desire to show my son that I was an involved parent, I raised my hand to volunteer to be head coach. Mind you, I knew very little about soccer. Baseball, football, basketball would have been different for sure, as I grew up playing all of these sports. My knowledge of soccer was pretty limited: I knew when a goal was scored, what a soccer ball looked like and the fact that a player could not use their hands (except for the goalie of course). Beyond that, I was clueless—a literal rank amateur of the game.

Now our second grade boys were a bunch of good, fun loving kids, but hard to corral at practices. Practices often devolved into an undisciplined frenzy that made it nearly impossible for my assistant

---

4   Teddy Roosevelt

coaches and me to instill any skill drills—what the heck, what did we know anyway?

When the season started, and much to our surprise, our boys' athleticism and energy overcame the incompetency of the coaching staff and our useless practices. Our little boys reeled off a fairly lengthy winning streak, usually trouncing their opponents handily. After a while, my assistant coaches and I decided to scrap practices all together. Practices were futile and for that matter, didn't seem to make a difference in the outcome of games.

One Saturday morning our undefeated team of boys showed up at the soccer field for its next scheduled game to face a team from a school we hadn't previously played. The opposing team had a coach who spoke with a British accent and obviously knew what he was doing, possessing a clear and obvious knowledge of the game of soccer. Furthermore, the coach put his players through a series of well-choreographed pre-game soccer drills. The disciplined, orderly and business-like approach to pre-game drills stood in sharp contrast to our team. The opposing team took their pre-game drills seriously and workmanlike. Meanwhile, over on our side of the practice field, our boys were scampering around in characteristically undisciplined fashion. Yeah, they looked like they were having a good time and seemed to genuinely enjoy each other, but whatever they were doing did not resemble the game of soccer. *Oh my*, I said to myself, we were facing the Manchester United of youth soccer while our boys were just goofing around! I turned to my two assistants and we all agreed we were about to have our "heads handed to us" and our winning streak was about to end. The only unknown was how lopsided a loss we would suffer.

After the whistle blew to start the match, the talent difference became apparent from the get-go. Our boys were much faster, more athletic and much more energetic than the opposing team (whom I had dubbed the Manchester United of youth soccer). It seemed like our boys were operating with eight cylinder engines and the kids on the other side operating with four. If my memory serves me well, our boys reeled off something like eight straight goals before the opponents managed to score a lucky goal. The final score was around 11-1 and could have been worse if I hadn't pulled my best players off the field early.

Right before the obligatory post-game hands shake, where players from both teams as well as the respective coaches line up to say nice things to each other in a demonstration of sportsmanship, I caught a glimpse of the opposing team's head coach. The look on his face spoke volumes—a look that said he was all too familiar with that day's outcome. Poor fellow, he just did not have talented players. No amount of coaching knowledge, no amount of repetition or well-choreographed soccer drills could make up for the lack of talent. For sure, our boys probably could have done better if they were better coached; but heck, why complain given the results?

Moral of the story: surround yourself with the best talent you can hire, motivate and retain.

The Successful CFO

One of the most important responsibilities of the CFO is to have a successor (or two or three...) in place. If a targeted successor is not immediately ready to step into the CFO's role, a development plan should be in place for this individual to be ready to be named CFO in a reasonably short period of time. The CFO should be able to look at his finance and accounting team and genuinely say that his or her successor is in place and either ready to step into the job or has the potential of becoming CFO in short order, with the proper mentoring. It's even better when the CFO can look at his organization and conclude he or she has multiple successors in place that have the potential of becoming CFO. Sometimes, a motivated, talented lieutenant will not wait for the CFO to leave or be promoted and gets recruited by another company needing a CFO. There may be some short-term pain associated with the departure of this individual and hopefully, there is someone in place to step into the vacated position. In any event, I would say that the CFO has done his or her job.

In fact, the CFO should insist that all of his or her direct reports have a succession plan in place. Many companies have well established human resource processes that make succession planning an important initiative of the organization. In fact, many boards of directors insist that a succession planning process is in place for all key executives. No matter if this is the case or not, the CFO should view succession planning as a priority leadership responsibility.

Talented, motivated, upwardly mobile staff makes the CFO's job and life easier. Allow me to cite some of the advantages, as they are numerous:

1. Talent, especially motivated subordinates, will often work harder and smarter and take some of the workload off the CFO. There is nothing wrong with the CFO working fewer hours. Furthermore, the more the CFO can get "out of the weeds", the better the CFO can focus on the issues and the initiatives that really matter to the company.

2. Many companies won't promote a CFO unless their successor is in place. This is good business practice. Why promote a CFO if it leaves a gap in a critical company leadership position that may have to be filled by a long, exhaustive outside search process? Many CFOs have their sights set on moving up the corporate ladder and many CFOs make good candidates to become CEO. It's always a good idea to have a successor in place.

3. No CFO has a monopoly on good ideas. I worked with a very sharp individual on my staff that I considered to be my "right-hand man" and whom I had pegged as my successor, and for very good reasons. This individual consistently brought to my attention intelligent, creative ideas to solve tricky financial issues—ideas that I would not have thought of on my own. Many of these ideas

were adopted and resulted in saving the company significant cash or worked the company out of tricky financial conundrums. In situations like this, "give credit where credit is due". That is, recognize the individual who came up with the idea. Make a big deal out of the successful idea and let it be known to key members of the company. Trust me; this will bolster your status within the company. You will look bigger rather than smaller despite the fact that it was someone else and not you who generated the great idea.

4. If your talented, motivated subordinates leave the company and become CFOs elsewhere, you will be rewarded in the long term. You want to be known as the CFO who populated the world with individuals whom you have groomed to become CFOs in other companies. Outsiders will notice and your stature will be enhanced. Executive recruiters will take note and place you on their list of candidates to consider for executive roles in other companies. Even if the CFO is not interested in being recruited outside the company, he or she will likely increase the number of other business and professional opportunities, such as Board of Directors' seats.

The CFO's direct reports often carry the titles of Controller, Chief Accounting Officer, Director of Internal Audit, Treasurer, Chief Information Officer, Chief Risk

Officer, Tax Director and many variations of these titles. A CFO should not be expected to become a subject matter expert for all the functional responsibilities that fall under his or her purview, nor should the CFO try to become a subject matter expert. The CFO should focus on hiring, retaining and motivating talented individuals who are subject matter experts.

By emphasizing the importance of recruiting and developing talent, I am not trying to diminish the significance of a properly functioning accounting and finance systems (see Chapter Five). Your company can have the most sophisticated financial and accounting systems in the world capable of producing an endless stream of financial data. However, if the right quality of human talent does not exist in your finance and accounting organization, then I guarantee you this financial data will not be properly "mined" or used as effective information that will add value to your company.

Don't be shy about paying up for talent either when hiring, even if it might "bust" the salary ranges that the company's human resource department established for its compensation program. If a clearly superior candidate (talent) has emerged out of an interviewing process but wants to be compensated higher than established compensation levels, the CFO needs to make the persuasive argument to hire this individual (again, this is where building key relationships comes in handy). I have never failed to convince the human resource folks to agree to make a departure from established compensation policies when it comes to hiring an exceptional individual.

The Successful CFO

When CFOs surround themselves with quality, motivated talent, delegation becomes an important exercise for the CFO. The CFO may have ascended to the position because he or she was very good at being a *doer*, but the CFO should be focused on analysis, leadership and strategy so they can become a **Positive Influencer**.

Now, I fully understand that the number of supporting staff reporting to the CFO varies depending upon organizational size. A smaller organization likely requires the CFO to still be engaged in a fair amount of doing. However, for most companies, if the CFO finds that they are still working on spreadsheets, they need to step back and question why. Certainly, there will be confidential or sensitive analyses that need to be prepared that are of such a confidential nature that the CFO should assume direct responsibility for preparation. Understood. Hopefully, these occasions are isolated.

The CFO should be entirely focused on developing and motivating talent and serving as a strategic partner to the CEO and the rest of the executive management team. The CFO's greatest tools are his or her brain, experience and leadership—not the keyboard.

"The job no leader should delegate----having the right people in the right place"[5]

---

5   Execution (2002), Larry Bossidy (former Chairman and CEO of Honeywell) and Ram Charan, executive advisor and author

Chapter 3

Translating Financial Information

The Successful CFO

Let me start this chapter with another life experience. I was recruited as CFO of another public company and when I arrived for my first day at work, the CEO announced to me that we were leaving town that night and presenting at an investor conference. Although I had done many investor conferences in the past, I felt a tad unprepared as I had just joined this particular company and had a lot to learn about the business. The CEO wanted to "throw me to the wolves", so to speak, undoubtedly to size up my communication approach and skills. We used the typical PowerPoint slides to deliver our presentation to investors. To be fair, he split up the presentation so that he would present the slides that described the business while I would focus on those slides that communicated financial information about the company.

So after we delivered the presentation, I asked the CEO for a critique of how well I did, hoping to receive some positive feedback. The CEO gave me feedback all right, but not necessarily the kind of feedback I was hoping to hear (albeit, delivered in the nicest way possible). Apparently, I could have done much better in his eyes. However, he gave me some enduring advice that I have taken to heart ever since. I have not only embraced this advice for myself but repeat it often when coaching subordinates when guiding them when communicating or presenting any financial information to co-workers, management or any audience for that matter, including investors, boards of directors, bankers, etc.

The CEO's advice went something like this. When you deliver a presentation about the company to an audience of investors *"...you are telling a story..."* and just not repeating bullet points on a slide. Mind you, I didn't exactly read the bullet points on the slides word for word, but I came awfully close to doing so.

"Telling a story" is not meant to suggest that you are articulating fiction, but instead "telling a story" is meant to develop a narrative that better illustrates what your company is all about.

As having been a member of the board of directors of several companies, I became accustomed to the routine of receiving board material in advance of the actual board meetings. A critical part of being a good board member is to read all the material received and be well prepared to ask appropriate questions of management when attending the board meetings in person.

One particular company for which I served on the board followed the normal routine of delivering a board book in advance of meetings; the board material always included the most recent monthly or quarterly financial statements along with supporting analysis. I would always read the material in advance, striving to be a well prepared board member, and would note the following, for example:

Sales were up 2%, year over year

Gross Margins declined 4%, year over year

Very interesting, I wondered what happened to cause these negative comparable results.

I would get to the board meeting, anxious to hear what management had to say about these numbers. As is typically the case, the CFO spoke to the financial data, analysis and financial statements included in the board material. When it came time to discuss the financials, the CFO went on to say the following:

"Sales were up 2%, year over year

Gross Margins declined 4%, year over year"

A rote recitation of what was already in the materials. Gee, Mr.[6] CFO, tell me something I don't already know. *Not very impressive, I muttered to myself*.

I reference back to Chapter One, transitioning from **Doer to Influencer** and the commentary regarding developing a deep and intimate knowledge of the business. If the CFO develops an intimate knowledge of the business, he or she can make the numbers come alive and provide some meaningful narrative (story) of what is going on in the business.

So what if the CFO would have described the above financial performance in the example I cited above in following manner instead?

"Quarter three's sales declined from the third quarter a year ago as the launch of Product XYZ was delayed due to supply chain issues. The supply chain issues were directly related to bottlenecks at our Kansas City distribution facility due to the inability of a key supplier to deliver the packaging material needed to deliver this product to our customers. You may re-

---

6   For this particular company, the CFO was male.

call that Product XYZ is an advanced version of our highly profitable Product RST, which we phased out in anticipation of the Product XYZ launch. The lack of sales of both RST and XYX, which would have been our highest margin products sold, is the reason for the decline in gross margins, which was impacted a full three percentage points from the lack of sales of both RST and XYZ products.

Going forward, we have now resolved the supply chain issues on Product XYZ and expect to see a full quarter's worth of sales for this new product. As the selling price point for Product XYZ is slightly higher than RST, while the cost of this product is virtually the same as Product RST, we expect gross margins to return to at least historic levels, if not higher in Quarter 4. Any questions…"

Now, Mr. or Ms. CFO, you're telling me something meaningful. Now, you've become more than a bean counter.

CFOs should approach the communication of any financial information using what I call the business narrative approach. Of course, the narrative needs to be factually true. The CFO should avoid using technical financial and accounting jargon, lest he or she comes off as the dreaded "bean counter". Save the accounting and finance jargon for the auditors or accounting geeks. Terms that the CFO consider native to his or her lexicon may sound "Greek" to the audience, particularly those individuals who don't possess any kind of financial education or background.

The Successful CFO

Almost every company has Audit Committees of their Board of Directors. CFOs are primarily responsible for communicating financial results and information to Audit Committees. The responsibilities of the Audit Committee are to provide oversight on the company's preparation of financial statements, along with overseeing the work of the auditors and the company's internal controls over the preparation of those financial statements.

I have had the distinct advantage of serving as a sitting CFO of a company while at the same time serving as a member of an Audit Committee for another company. I fully appreciate both roles and responsibilities and how they differ. Furthermore, I have developed a fair amount of empathy for the responsibilities of an Audit Committee member and have made it a goal to facilitate their ability to perform their responsibilities.

As a CFO, I learned to start off every Audit Committee meeting with a brief business overview of what transpired in the company the prior quarter. This brief business overview would usually take no more than ten minutes with the express purpose of providing some meaningful background on what occurred in the business before the Audit Committee would dive into the financial statements. Although I would script out this business overview, I would never read it word for word. The script was written to merely help me develop the narrative to make it easier to communicate my understanding of what happened in the business for the period of time discussed. I believed communicating this brief business overview provided context and meaning to the raw numbers that the Audit Committee would review. An attempt to make the numbers "come alive".

This is an approach that a CFO could use for any internal or external communication of financial information.

Let me go back to the original story line in this chapter—the presentation of my company to investors (and other external stakeholders for that matter).

Communicating with investors and other external stakeholders, such as bankers, is a key job responsibility for CFOs. It is important for the CFO to demonstrate that he or she has an intimate knowledge of their business and is not merely a financial wonk (bean counter). It is important for the CFO to communicate not only what the company does for a living and the financial results, but also to communicate the following:

- Why does your company exist?

- What value does your company bring to its customers, clients, etc.

- What differentiates your company from the competition?

- Why should an existing investor stay an investor, or a potential investor want to invest? (Be careful with this one. You never want to appear to be over – selling your company. If you can articulate an investment case for the first three bullets enumerated above, you've essentially accomplished this bullet point as well).

The above points need to be communicated in as understated a manner as possible; a CFO earns more credibility when his or her company financially delivers on its message. Overselling your company is typically not well received by external stakeholders. As CFO, your job is to credibly educate and inform, not to sell. Let your company's performance speak for itself.

Before presenting to investors (and other external stakeholders), step back and think about the two or three important messages you want the audience to walk away with and remember. Focus on those two or three messages and insure that your business narrative is delivered in a clear, concise and persuasive—but understated—fashion.

Chapter 4

Managing the Balance Sheet

> *"Cash is king. Get every drop of cash you can get and hold onto it"*[7]

Balance Sheet or Income Statement? Where should the CFO focus more of his or her time and attention? In my humble opinion, this is a no-brainer: The balance sheet, and it all starts with the management and forecasting of cash and cash flow. The entire management of the balance sheet is important for the CFO to steward. However, there are four areas I believe every CFO should focus their attention:

- Cash (forecasting)

- Liquidity

- Capital Formation

- Accounts Receivable

All four of these areas are interrelated and ultimately lead back to cash.

Cash (Forecasting)

> *"I've never known a CFO that was fired for having too much cash on hand[8]"*

If you're the CFO of Apple or Coca-Cola, perhaps the management of cash flow is less important as these enterprises are literally cash flow generating machines. Last time I checked, Apple had nearly $70 billion of cash and short term investments on its

---

7   Jack Welch, former Chairman and CEO of General Electric
8   Myself

balance sheet and continues to generate a fountain of operating cash flow every quarter. The biggest challenge CFOs of enterprises such as Apple and Co-ca-Cola probably face is how to best invest the huge treasury of cash their respective companies possess and generate on an ongoing basis and to efficiently manage the tax consequences of holding this cash in various jurisdictions. Such a nice problem!

Most of us CFOs are not that fortunate to work for companies like Apple or Coca-Cola.

Again, allow me to start with a personal experience that drove home the importance of cash management.

Earlier in my career, I worked as the CFO of a business unit of a major energy services company. Whilst I was responsible for balance sheet management of this business unit, I really never worried about whether we had enough cash on hand to run our operations and make our capital investments. When we needed cash to fund capital investments, we just rang up "sugar daddy corporate" and as long as the capital investment was approved in the annual budget, the cash magically showed up in our business unit's account.

Several years later I was appointed CFO of a public company. I immediately noted that the company did not perform any granular level of cash forecasting other than as a byproduct of big picture business models which were earnings driven. I wasn't too worried as the treasury department supplied me with a "Daily Cash Report", telling me how much money sat in our various bank accounts for the previous working day. I looked at these reports each day, noted that we had hundreds of millions of dollars in our bank accounts and did not worry any further. I was lulled into complacency.

A few months after I arrived at this company, a confluence of adverse external events occurred impacting our business. Shortly thereafter, I began to see the amounts showing up in our "Daily Cash Report" start to trend downward each day. As the days, weeks and months marched on, the amount of cash on hand seemed to spiral downward at an alarming rate.

I quickly realized that I was literally steering the financial ship of the company blind. I had no idea how much cash the company would have on hand tomorrow, or a week later, a month later or six months later for that matter. One day, upon receiving the Daily Cash Report showing a precipitous day to day drop in our cash balances, I walked into our CEOs office and declared "we are running out of cash". Furthermore, we were literally tapped out on our revolving credit facility. There was no "deep pockets sugar daddy" corporate to call up for an emergency injection of cash. Due to the confluence of external events, it was not feasible to access the capital markets either.

The old proverb applied here: *"Necessity is the mother of invention"*.

We immediately sprang into action and implemented a robust weekly cash flow forecasting system. We required every business unit in every part of the world we operated to submit a detailed rolling thirteen week cash flow forecast, which would be updated on a weekly basis. We held the business units accountable to submit their reports each Monday at a set time, regardless of the time zone a particular business unit resided. Now when I say system, the report was actually prepared and submitted on Microsoft Excel™ and consolidated based on the features embedded within the Excel program. All it took was someone on our staff literate in Excel to install the macros needed for an efficient and timely consolidation of the various business unit cash flow forecasts. The sum total to implement: $0.00.

Once we received the first report, we had a good starting point on cash coming in and going out the door, so to speak. From there, we had the requisite information to develop an action plan to improve our cash position and ultimately the company was financially stabilized.

In addition to the weekly cash flow forecast report, we developed a "waterfall" style report to provide us a snapshot of how well we were doing at cash flow forecasting. I have attached a sample report in the Appendix to illustrate what I mean by the waterfall nature of the report. This allowed us to determine quickly, over a number of weeks, if we were forecasting too aggressively or too conservatively with the ability to isolate by business unit. If a business unit missed their cash flow forecast for a particular week by an amount that was more than minor, either plus or minus, the financial individual responsible for the report received a call from corporate asking to explain the variance. If a particular business unit was consistently conservative or aggressive, serious discussions would take place with the responsible person.

The company became really good at forecasting cash for a thirteen week look forward, but we knew that thirteen weeks was not quite a long enough time horizon. Ultimately, we stretched out the forecasting to twenty six weeks. The data that went into the development of these reports was intended to be very granular; business units needed to identify specific receivables scheduled for collection, the actual accounts payable invoices that would clear the bank, tax payments and payroll related outlays, etc. for each week in the twenty six week forecast. Obviously, the further out a particular week was forecasted, the less accuracy could be expected of the forecast. Nonetheless, we asked our finance and accounting company to make a serious, thoughtful attempt to forecast as accurately as possible. I question the validity of extending this type of very granular forecasting beyond twenty six weeks, as again, accuracy is naturally more and more difficult to master the longer out one forecasts.

I received the weekly cash flow forecast like clockwork every Monday evening. To emphasize the importance of this report to me, I would constantly repeat and declare to the rest of the organization that the most important financial report generated for me, as CFO, was the weekly cash flow forecast. The company's accounting system used an Oracle ERP system which cost millions to implement (it functioned well and I'm sure the business unit personnel responsible for the weekly cash flow forecast used data from Oracle in the preparation of the forecast), however, it is interesting to note that the most valuable report for me was implemented on a Microsoft Excel spreadsheet.

Liquidity

"I've been rich and I've been poor -- and believe me, rich is better"[9]

I've worked for companies that had too much liquidity at times and too little at other times – believe me too much is better. Well, that is if you believe that there is such a thing as having too much liquidity. In my humble opinion, a company can never have too much liquidity.

I define liquidity to be unrestricted cash on hand (or cash-like instruments) plus amounts available under revolving credit (or working capital) facilities. Cash is the primary, most valuable source of liquidity. However, revolving credit facilities should be an important element of liquidity as well.

I have never known a situation where a CFO was fired for having "too much" cash. Certainly, companies which carry lots of cash on hand and have a consistent track record of generating free cash flow probably return a fair amount of cash to investors, either in the form of dividends and/ or share repurchases. I firmly believe that companies that have a

---

9   Sophie Tucker, actress

mature or maturing business profile with a proven long-term history of sustainable free cash flow generation should return excess cash on hand to shareholders. *Note: As a personal investment strategy, I don't invest in very many companies that don't pay dividends.*

There is no simple rule of thumb on how much liquidity any company should have. Every company has a different financial profile and business model. Investment grade[10] companies have much broader, less expensive sources of financing (such as commercial paper) than non-investment grade companies which may lessen the need for having—relatively—lots of liquidity.

I've worked nearly my entire career in the energy industry, a highly cyclical industry. When the cycle turns up, it seems as if the industry generates a substantial amount of cash flow. When the cycle turns down, the industry burns through cash at a precipitous rate. I have often been criticized by investors during up cycles, when liquidity was seemingly at very high levels, to more aggressively invest the money for business expansion or to return cash to shareholders in the form of share repurchases. I would find the criticism amusing. I didn't know when the up cycle would turn down, but experience taught me that a down turn was inevitable. I've learned that when the cycle did turn down, the company would benefit, if not survive the down cy-

---

10   A debt instrument is considered investment grade if its credit rating is BBB- or higher by Standard & Poor's or Baa3 or higher by Moody's

cle, from having a starting point of "excess liquidity", which ultimately proved not to be excess liquidity after all.

I have never had the good fortune or luxury of serving as the CFO of an investment grade company. If this applies to your situation as well, I believe it is the responsibility of the CFO to insure that his or her company has a (very) safe level of liquidity on hand.

Recall the definition of liquidity: unrestricted cash (plus cash equivalents) plus availability under revolving credit (working capital) facilities. Revolving credit facilities are great, but cash on hand is better. Cash is always king.

I'm a big fan of revolving credit facilities secured from a commercial bank or bank group. While not a permanent source of capital, revolving credit facilities can serve to deal with short-term cash shortfalls needed to operate your company due to seasonal factors or if your company has a lumpy revenue profile. They are also useful as a short term funding mechanism when making acquisitions until more permanent sources of capital are obtained, if needed. Many revolving credit facilities are secured along with short term loans and typically mature in three to five years. Combined, I will call revolving credit facilities and bank term loans as "credit facilities".

Why am I a big fan?

- These credit facilities are usually secured as a result of a relationship building exercise between the company, with the CFO as the point person, and the bank(s). Most of the relationships involve local banking officials even if the bank itself is not based near the home office of the company. (*Yeah, isn't it funny how so many aspects of the CFO's responsibilities go back to relationship building?*)

- Credit facilities usually carry lower interest rates than many other types of debt instruments. This is due to the fact that most credit facilities are secured by assets of the company pledged as collateral and have maturities that are relatively short term in nature.

Credit facilities almost always have restrictive and maintenance covenants: e.g., maximum leverage ratio, fixed charge coverage ratio, limits on capital expenditures; restrictions on asset dispositions, the payment of dividends, share repurchases, and so on and so forth. I would argue that these covenants represent prudent financial guideposts which companies should adhere to even if a credit facility were not in existence. Non-compliance with a covenant or restriction potentially puts the loan in default with damaging consequences to the company.

The loan documents that govern these facilities are so complex and lengthy that they would make a reader go cross-eyed trying to understand. After all, they are written by lawyers. It's not unusual for a CFO to find out that their company is out of compliance with a particular provision of the loan document.

Although credit facilities are complex and easy to fall out of compliance with, I am still a big fan. *Why*?

As opposed to other forms of debt securities, when the CFO finds the company out of compliance, he or she can actually speak with a real person; hopefully, a bank officer with whom the company and the CFO have hopefully developed a good relationship. Other forms of debt securities are held by institutional investors who may hold the "paper" one day and then trade it to another investor the next day. It is difficult for the CEO to develop any kind of meaningful working relationship with individuals or investors who hold these types of loans.

Banks and bankers only want to declare a loan in default in the most egregious of situations or when they lose confidence in management's ability to manage the financial affairs of the company, thus jeopardizing the repayment of their loans. Banks are very reluctant to assume financial control of a company and only in situations where they feel taking direct control of the collateral is better than allowing the company to continue to manage the assets that represent the collateral. If the CFO has well developed relationships and has earned the confidence of the banks, the banks will perceive the CFO as an individual who provides a steady hand to the financial stewardship of the company. The banks will almost always work with the company to waive the non-compliant provision, either temporarily or permanently (for a relatively minor fee).

Don't get me wrong, in no way am I saying that credit facilities are the only form of debt that a company should consider. However, having an unfunded revolving credit facility aspect adds another layer of liquidity for the company.

Capital Formation

Just as I've never known a CFO that was fired for having too much cash on hand, I've never known a company that regretted raising equity. Existing shareholders may be critical of the dilution that ensues from an equity capital raise. However, over the course of time, companies that have not been afraid of raising equity usually survive if not thrive. I'm not at all suggesting that companies raise equity indiscriminately. However, companies should constantly run sensitivity models on their company's financial forecasts, paying particular attention to downside scenarios. If the CFO doesn't like what he or she sees in those downside scenarios, then consider pushing for capital formation through equity raises, particularly when capital market conditions are conducive and your company has the ability to access the capital markets. I'm not saying there is not a place for debt in your company's capital structure, particularly if your company has a relatively low net debt-to-book capitalization[11] profile. Again, nothing wrong with debt, but there is a limit to how much debt a company should put on its balance sheet.

I don't know too many CFOs that were fired for having too much cash, or CFOs that regretted raising

---

11   Net debt to book capitalization is defined as gross debt, less cash on hand to total capitalization, which is net debt plus shareholders' equity.

equity, but I sure know companies that found themselves in financial distress or even bankruptcy when they found themselves with not enough cash to satisfy their debt obligations. Many CFOs lost their jobs in these situations.

Lehman Brothers, Pacific Gas and Electric, Peabody Energy, Sports Authority and WorldCom are all well-known companies that either no longer exist or declared bankruptcy. Undoubtedly, a variety of factors influenced the demise of these businesses, but I have to believe if the capital structure of these companies was much more tilted to equity versus debt, the outcome may have been different.

Think equity. No restrictive covenants, no principal amortization, no interest payments, no maturities. Yeah, yeah, I can't tell you how many times the smart financial types have told me that equity is the most expensive form of capital. I get their point. Think equity anyway.

Accounts Receivable

"Tell me how you measure me, and I will tell you how I behave."[12]

Sales and marketing personnel for any company are wired and innately motivated to generate and grow sales. Most companies' incentive programs reward sales personnel for making and increasing sales. I have never met a sales person that wasn't top line focused. Sales and marketing personnel will often push the boundaries of good business practices in

---

12   Dr. Eliyahu M. Goldratt

order to generate sales. Don't get me wrong, over the years I have learned to admire the value of sales and marketing personnel. I have found that most possess an incredibly deep knowledge of the business and the products and services they sell. They are indispensable to the success and vitality of most businesses.

It is incumbent upon the CFO of the company to develop appropriate credit policies to establish the guideposts so that the enthusiasm of sales and marketing personnel can be channeled appropriately.

Trust me, accounts receivable write-offs and bad debt reserves will always reflect poorly upon the CFO, regardless of whether the decision to sell to a particularly bad credit was the idea of the sales and marketing team. Boards of Directors and other stakeholders will wonder why the appropriate controls were not established to prevent these occurrences. The CFO will be primarily looked at for the failure of the company to prevent bad debts.

I realize that the CFO cannot do it alone, so to speak. Leadership on the part of the CEO is often necessary to establish the right sales and marketing culture. Again, reference back to Chapter One and the critical importance of establishing relationships with the CEO and other key members of the company.

There are a couple of axioms I have often preached to the sales and marketing force. I hope you find them useful:

"You can't spend accounts receivable, but you sure can spend cash"

-and-

"A sale does not derive any economic benefit to the company until it is converted to cash"

Developing credit acceptance policies that are sensible, which don't overly restrict the ability of the company to generate and grow sales, is a crucial responsibility of the CFO and his staff. These policies need to be broadly communicated to the organization as a whole, and more specifically to sales and marketing personnel. Again, having the clear and demonstrable support of the CEO cannot be understated.

The credit policy should have a multi-layered approach that divides customers into various credit quality levels. For example:

Category A: well established and well-known customers that have public financial information available that clearly establishes a healthy financial position

For these customers, the extension of credit should be automatic and on cruise control.

Category B: Customers that are not that well known or don't have public information available, but have an established track record of doing business with your company and a demonstrated track record of timely payment of accounts receivable.

Customers in this category should have credit granted automatically, but a constant review process should be established.

Category C: Existing customers that have not demonstrated a track of timely payment of accounts receivable or prospective customers that do not fit Category A.

For existing customers that have proven to be "problem payers", but where a strategic rationale exists for continuing the granting of credit, sales and finance should clearly collaborate. Nevertheless, finance should carry a heavy weighting in the credit decision.

Category D: Customers that are known to be derelict payers or companies that present financial information that reveals a serious inability to pay. For customers or potential customers in this category, a decision needs to be made as to whether the company sells only upon the receipt of cash, letter of credit, or some other form of collateral.

Again, the above is merely an over-simplified outline; the purpose of which is to stress the importance of having a credit review process.

The faster a company converts accounts receivable to cash, the healthier that company will be financially.

The most important effort exerted in collecting accounts receivable occurs before the invoice is mailed to the customer, client, etc. Above, I discussed credit policies which are critical in minimizing collection efforts associated with slow payers or bad credits. But an equally important effort is associated with getting the invoice correct before it's ever mailed.

I can't tell you how many times a customer, even those that are timely payers, hold back payment because an invoice was incorrectly prepared. Sometimes the errors involved represent a very small fraction of the overall invoice value. Many times, invoices list items that were billed at prices or rates that were not consistent with previously agreed upon prices and rates. These problems are, more often than not, self-inflicted, wasting the time and energy of not only accounting personnel in attempting to resolve the errors, but also of sales personnel who are required to become involved with customers in an attempt to sort out the error.

The CFO should lead the charge for process improvement in the invoicing/accounts receivable area.

Chapter 5

Generating Timely Financial Information

Generating timely financial information that is meaningful for the organization is a critical success factor for the CFO. The CFO should focus on the following in order to achieve this success factor:

1. Timely and efficient closing of the books of the company and the generation of financial statements.

2. Forecasting—particularly short-term forecasting.

Closing the Books

There is an old cliché that goes something like this:

"You don't know where you are going until you know where you have been."

Applying this quote to the subject of closing the books: if it takes you too long to figure out where you have been, how are you supposed to make timely adjustments to where you are going?

I have served on the board of directors of a few companies and have different experiences when it comes to the timely distribution of financial information. For example, for one particular company I would show up at board meetings in the first or second week of August, having just received the June/Quarter Two financial results a day or two before the meeting. It was obvious to me that the accounting function for this particular company was struggling closing the books and producing the financial statements. I would attend the Audit Committee meeting to find out that a few adjustments to financial statements were still in process and the numbers were not yet finalized. The difficulties that the accounting team experienced were confirmed by comments made by the external auditors. This particular company consistently struggled to meet the financial statement filing deadlines required under SEC reporting rules.

Obviously, the accounting function did not have its act together. The CFO bears responsibility for the fact that this environment exists. How can a company effectively manage its business if it takes 40 plus days after the fact to determine its financial results for any given period? How can management react and take corrective action in a timely fashion?

If your company does not close its books in five business days or less, something's wrong. I'm not saying that an adjustment or two might have to be booked to the financials after these five days, but a company should have a fairly good idea of its prior period's financial results in five business days or less. I will argue that a company should already have a clear idea of its financial results for any given month (period) well in advance of the close of that month. See discussion below on forecasting.

Here are some observations I have developed over the years regarding the accounting close cycle:

- A company that closes their books quickly seems to produce more accurate financial information vis-à-vis companies which take far longer to close their books. The "quick closers" seem to have much fewer "late minute" adjustments and internal control weaknesses. Less effort seems to be exerted by the auditors and that saves money.

- The finance and accounting staff of companies that close their books quickly are far less stressed and work fewer hours. Again, nothing wrong with working fewer hours. Working smarter is better than working harder.

- When the finance and accounting team can close the books quickly, more time can be devoted by the team in analyzing financial information for the management team—an exercise that adds real value to their companies.

- It's much easier to retain finance and accounting staff (talent) when these human resources are not in a constant cycle of burning the midnight oil. All things being equal, why work for a company that requires you to work 60 plus hours a week, when you can work 40 hours a week somewhere else?

Certainly, having standardized accounting or ERP systems, such as SAP, Oracle, Microsoft Dynamics, Sage or Quick Books, et al. for that matter, are helpful. Standardized accounting processes and procedures across the company are facilitated by having everyone on the same accounting platform. However, to achieve the goal of closing the books in five days or less, it often takes more than just an expensive accounting software system. It takes a mindset and the proper approach.

Here are some ideas on how your company can achieve a five day closing cycle:

- Consider adopting a "soft close" approach for the interim months of any quarterly period. Most stakeholders are focused on quarterly results. Certainly, public companies must report quarterly results on a 10Q, and these results must be accurate. However, interim results (July and August for instance) don't bear the same level of consequences for accuracy as quarterly results. Auditors, audit committees, the SEC, and shareholders for that matter are focused on quarterly results. If you can get the interim months of a quarter more or less ninety-five percent accurate, that should be good enough in my opinion.

  CFOs should analyze the amount of effort required to move from 95% accuracy to 100% accuracy for interim months and question the purpose in engaging in the processes required to achieve the incremental 5% accuracy. Freeing up time to focus on quarterly results and financial analysis will serve your company much better. In a soft close, you might consider reducing the effort required to perform the following for interim months:

- o Depreciation expense. You should calculate depreciation expense at the start of each quarter and book a repetitive entry each month, truing up only for quarterly results. Your accounting policies should provide you the flexibility of not having to book depreciation expense for mid-month acquisitions of long-lived assets.

- o Do revenue and expense accruals really need to be booked in interim months?

- o Consider performing account reconciliations on a quarterly basis only.

- o Standardize recurring entries for overhead allocations and true up only on a quarterly basis.

I am sure CFOs and their staffs can add to the list above.

- Intercompany transactions should have well-established accounting policies and practices. Many companies operate across several stand-alone business units and/or across various legal entities which require separate stand-alone financial statements for each reporting unit that are then consolidated each month. Typically, these companies engage in intercompany transactions. One of the more frustrating situations accounting teams have is the existence of an imbalance in intercompany accounts when financial statements are consolidated. Reconciling these imbalances seems to take an inordinate amount of staff effort and if the imbalances are significant, could hold up the release of the financial statements. Auditors will spend very expensive time trying to understand the materiality and impact of these imbalances to the company's consolidated financial statements. There is no value added whatsoever to an organization that finds itself with this condition. What a waste of precious time and resources, both human and financial.

This condition does not need to exist. No reporting unit should be permitted to book an intercompany transaction unless the other reporting unit books it simultaneously, and I mean at exactly the same time. Companies that have standardized accounting systems across the enterprise usually embed internal controls to insure the simultaneous booking of intercompany transactions. Even if your company does not have all reporting units on the same standardized accounting system, firmly established accounting policies and procedures should be in place or implemented to insure that intercompany accounting transactions are recorded simultaneously.

One other practice to consider is to "cut-off" the recording of intercompany transactions a few days before the close of any accounting period. This allows the accounting department to insure that no intercompany imbalances exist facilitating the efficient closing of the books. Auditors need be onboard. Another practice is to automatically allow the reporting unit initiating the intercompany transaction to cause the other reporting unit(s) to have to book the transaction. Intercompany disputes can be sorted out after the fact.

- Unnecessary, low value reports or seldom used reports. The typical accounting and finance function produces a large quantity of financial information and data for various constituents in their respective organizations. For every company I have ever worked for, it never fails that I discover reports that are produced that the recipient either doesn't look at or sits in the recipient's in box for days or weeks on end after the report is prepared only to be immediately transferred to "File 13" once picked up. Often these reports were "one-off" requests that somehow became routinely generated. Even if the report is not trashed, one has to question the value of a report that is not quickly read by a recipient.

The CFO should identify all reports produced by the accounting and finance staff and determine those that are either low value or rarely read by recipients and stop the production of these reports. Sure, the CFO should have a discussion with the recipient of these reports and reach consensus that these reports no longer need to be produced. My experience has shown that the recipient usually agrees or can be easily persuaded.

The benefits of such an exercise are limitless. Staff morale should be improved. I don't know too many individuals who like working on non-productive activities. As importantly, freeing up the accounting and finance staff to focus their attention on those activities (reports) that are meaningful to the company will only enhance the value of the function. Furthermore, the elimination of "useless reports" should streamline the accounting and financial reporting process significantly.

Forecasting

"If you have to forecast, forecast often."[13]

In the previous section of this chapter, I commented on the value of closing the books quickly in order for a company to know their historical financial performance. Only then can the management team make the necessary tactical adjustments to its business in a timely manner. However, I will argue that a company should have a fairly accurate idea, for example, of

---

13   Edgar Fiedler, American economist

June's results, not after the books are closed, but as soon as early June. The closing of the books should merely be an affirmation of what the company's forecasting system predicted within a fairly narrow range.

Most companies engage in monthly, quarterly, annual and multi-year forecasting. This exercise should be a cross-functional collaboration; i.e. the responsibility and collaboration of the sales, manufacturing, finance, etc. functions.

Short-term forecasting (monthly and quarterly) should be fairly precise. A forecast prepared in early June for the month of June should closely mirror the actual financial results of the company when the books are closed in early July, as an example.

Public companies typically provide the investment community with earnings guidance. Credible earnings guidance cannot be provided unless a robust and proven forecasting system is employed by the company. Reliable earnings guidance engenders credibility for the Company and the CFO.

Routine short-term forecasting is good management practice. For any given year, short-term forecasting begins with the development of an annual budget, ideally on a "bottoms-up" basis and before the start of any fiscal year. Bottoms-up means that every business unit that has profit and loss responsibility should submit an annual budget for which the business unit takes ownership. For sure the budget will likely be subject to input and changes from upper management, but the culmination of the process should leave the business unit (or cost centers in the case of administrative functions) with a strong feeling that they own the budget.

Thereafter, and as each month of the fiscal year goes by, the short-term forecast, which started as a budget, should be revised on a rolling twelve months basis. For example, a company with a December 31 fiscal year ending in, let's say 2019, should be forecasting 11 months into 2020 by the time November of 2019 rolls around. By doing so, the budgeting process for 2020 is made so much easier as the business unit (cost center) has already developed a forecast of almost all of 2020. An annual budget is merely a more formal presentation of the following fiscal year that is submitted to upper management and usually serves to set incentive compensation objectives.

This may sound like a lot of short term forecasting, but to the extent forecasting becomes a routine, high priority exercise, combined with a healthy dose of executive level sponsorship, then I believe that each month the forecast is updated turns into a relatively easy exercise. In order for "relatively easy" to be achieved, so that the recurring forecasting does not become an overly intrusive exercise for the company, forecasting accuracy should strive for and accept a +/- 5% target, with greater accuracy for forecasting three months out, and gradually less accuracy for months further out in the 12 month rolling period. With the proper emphasis, decent financial systems and a practical accuracy target (e.g., +/-95%), the personnel needed to complete this exercise should spend one day or less to complete and submit each month.

PricewaterhouseCoopers (PwC) issued an excellent study, titled *Financial Planning: Realizing the value of budgeting and forecasting*[14] on the subject of budgeting and forecasting in May of 2011. I would encourage the reader who is interested in a more in depth discussion of the subject to obtain a copy of this study.

The basis of longer term, multi-year forecasting should begin with the short-term forecasts developed, and can be some combination of a bottoms-up and a top-down approach. Longer term forecasting is inherently less reliable. That is why in my opinion; the CFO and the company should devote more of their time and effort in refining the short-term forecasting process.

---

14   Published by CFO Publishing LLC in May 2011, as funded by PwC

Chapter Six

Be Careful with these Activities

The first five chapters of this book outline the factors on which a CFO should put his or her focus that when mastered, should serve as the ingredients for becoming a successful CFO.

Obviously, there are many activities that call for the CFO's attention. There are three activities that I would like to specifically address to which the CFO should be careful about devoting too much time and attention:

1. Deal making

2. Investor relations

3. Dealing with the auditors (in a confrontational way)

Deal-making

Most CFOs are at the forefront of evaluating and negotiating strategic transactions; mergers, acquisitions and divestitures. There is a sort of adrenalin rush that results in being involved in the middle of these transactions. In many instances, big dollars are at stake and the consequences to the company for success or failure of these transactions are often significant. CFOs will likely work with investment bankers who have brought strategic transaction ideas to the company and/or have been engaged to advise the company on these strategic transactions.

My advice to the CFO is to be cautious and ever skeptical. Investment bankers are some of the smartest, most well-educated individuals with whom I have ever had the pleasure of working. They often bring a perspective to the company that might not otherwise be apparent to the CEO and the CFO. After all, the CEO and executive management team should be focused on the day to day activities of running the business and the CFO, the finance and accounting function. However, investment bankers are usually only compensated if a strategic transaction is ultimately culminated. Thus, they are not necessarily perfectly aligned to act in the best interests of the company. Sure, investment bankers will wine and dine you at the finest places in town. This can be very intoxicating (no pun intended).

Now, don't get me wrong, investment bankers can and should serve a very useful role as advisors to the company. They are indispensable when it comes to raising capital in the debt and equity markets. At one time in my career, I started up a mergers and acquisition advisory firm[15] licensed by the Financial Industry Regulatory Authority (a.k.a FINRA) to deal in securities related transactions, including raising capital for my clients. Essentially, I was as an investment banker at that time. I fully appreciate the contribution that investment bankers make to their clients and the financial markets.

Although there is a time and place for strategic transactions, the CFO should be careful about getting too caught up in the glory of deal making. The CFO adds real value in working with the executive management team in running the day to day business. There may be a time and place where a strate-

---

15   Arch Creek Advisors LLC

gic transaction complements or otherwise adds real value to the company. However, particularly when it comes to acquisitions, the CFO needs to adopt a cautious, if not skeptical mindset.

Investor Relations

A CFO of a public company is often perceived by the investment community (investors, potential investors, research analysts, the sales force of investment firms) as the second most critical member of management after the CEO. The CFO is expected to interact with the investment community and represent his or her company well. The investment community will quickly develop a perception of the CFO. Hopefully, this perception inspires confidence by the investment community.

Investor relations encompass many activities, including:

- Presentation of the company at investor conferences (often involving a slide show presentation and meetings with investors and potential investors)

- Working with industry research analysts

- Non-deal road shows where an investment firm arranges for executive management to meet with investors and/or potential investors

- Ad hoc meetings and phone calls with investors/potential investors

- Quarterly earnings conference calls

The first time I was appointed CFO of a publicly traded company, I was responsible for activities I previously did not have to worry about, including investor relations. A few months after my appointment, the CEO called me into his office and sternly declared that "...I was spending too much time on investor relations stuff..." The CEO admonished me, citing the activities that delivered real value to the company. My pitiful attempt to defend myself was not received very well and I recall leaving his office with a few mental scars and bruises. Although it was painful advice and I didn't like the feedback at the time, the CEO was absolutely correct. This particular CEO was the founder of the company, built the business from the ground up and grew it to the point where the company was taken public. He deeply understood what it took to build real value and truly appreciated the benefits of having a company which was publicly traded.

Hopefully, your company has a dedicated investor relations individual or function that can absorb much of the activities associated with investor relations. The CEO and CFO will still be expected to represent their companies for the various activities enumerated above, even when their companies have dedicated investor relations resources. Some investors insist on meeting or communicating with either the CEO or the CFO and not just the investor relations function.

The CFO needs to be careful with devoting too much of his or her time and energy to investor relations activities. Trust me, the CFO will be asked or invited to participate in investor relations activities which can consume much more time than should be allocated. Similar to my comments about investment bankers, investor relations activities can be tempting and glamourous.

For example, non-deal road show meetings often involve the sponsoring firm providing limousine service to and from each and every meeting. The CFO gets treated as royalty. The dinners are often at top notch restaurants and fine wine is often poured. Despite the royal treatment, over the years, I have found non-deal roadshows to be a form of necessary drudgery.

Similarly, with investor conferences. The executive management teams presenting at these conferences are treated like rock stars. These conferences are often held at five star hotels or luxury resorts.

I fully understand that once a company becomes public, or otherwise has publicly traded securities, investor relations become an integral part of the CFO's job description. All I am saying is to be careful about the amount of precious time you devote to these activities. Hopefully, you have a dedicated investor relations function that can help manage this activity for you (and the CEO).

Again, the CFO delivers real value in working with the executive leadership team to manage and grow their companies. When it comes to investor relations, keep this in mind: you can spend a lot of time meeting with investors, analysts, etc. However, in the end, your company's financial results speak the loudest.

The "sell-side" (research analysts and brokers of investment banking firms) will encourage (pressure) the CFO to meet with their clients, often in the form of wanting to take the CFO (and the CEO for that matter) on the road (see discussion of non-deal road shows above). I guarantee you that the amount of requests and the time that would be devoted to these requests, will exceed the amount of time prudent or necessary for the CFO to allocate to these exercises. A certain amount of these activities are okay and certainly the CFO needs to be cognizant of supporting the research analysts who write research on the company. All I am saying is that the CFO should not get caught up devoting too much time to these undertakings.

Dealing with the Auditors

Almost every organization has their financial statements audited by an independent auditing firm. The auditing world changed dramatically with the creation of the Public Company Accounting Oversight Board (PCAOB), by the Sarbanes-Oxley Act of 2002. The PCAOB was created in response to what was perceived to be auditor miss-steps in the wake of various accounting scandals, particularly associated with Enron and WorldCom. Whereas the industry was self-regulated prior to Sarbanes-Oxley, the PCAOB subjects auditors to independent, external oversight, including a rigorous inspection of the audit practices of the auditing firms. I understand that these inspections are far from pleasant (understatement) and no audit partner affixing his or her opinion on the financial statements of a company looks forward to having the audit of that company selected for inspection by the PCAOB. As a CFO of companies before and after the creation of the PCAOB, the change in approach and attitude by auditing firms has changed dramatically. I will not express an opinion as to whether this has been a change for the good or not.

Inevitably, management and auditors will come to a disagreement on the accounting treatment of certain transactions. My advice to CFOs: don't waste too much time or effort on trying to persuade the auditors to the company's way of thinking. My experience has shown that in the **vast majority** of these disagreements, the auditors won't budge. Auditors are more worried about what the PCAOB will think more so than what their clients think. It's the world we live in today. Every hour spent by the auditors in listening to management's point of view or reading management's memo as to why their conclusion is correct, is a wasted hour and as most of you know, auditors are expensive. Spending time arguing with auditors is of no economic benefit to the company.

If the CFO believes the accounting for a particular transaction falls in that gray area of interpretation but has a preferred accounting treatment, by all means document the basis for management's conclusion. Cite chapter and verse of accounting literature and present a memorandum to the auditors. Hopefully, the auditors agree, but if they don't, keep this in mind before deciding to press the issue any further: your chances of changing the auditor's mind is very low. However, win or lose, the company will incur incremental audit fees that derive no economic value to the company.

In Summary

The Successful CFO

There is no rocket science expressed in this book. The ingredients which make a CFO successful are fairly simple and can be summarized as follows:

- Develop strategic relationships both inside and outside your company. These relationships will help facilitate the CFOs ability to achieve all of the success factors discussed in this book.

- Surround yourself with the best talent you can possibly hire and retain. The CFOs ability to perform at a high level is impossible unless he or she is surrounded by good talent. Absent talent, the CFO will become immersed in the weeds and not be able to function at the strategic partnership level with the CEO and peers.

- Form an intimate understanding of your company's business which will enhance your ability to translate the financial results of your company to stakeholders in a meaningful, coherent manner. The CFO's efforts to understand the business will help in relationship building as well.

- Manage the balance sheet, particularly cash. Insure that your company has more than adequate cash resources for now and for the future. The CFO should insure that his or her company has liquidity levels representing a wide enough safety moat for the organization to withstand unexpected external events as well as company specific failures related from both the lack of execution on strategy or unexpected operational hiccups.

- Communicate and translate financial information to any audience, employing a business narrative. Avoid using accounting and finance nomenclature. Don't come across as a bean counter.

- Insure that the financial results of the company are developed on a timely basis and disseminated accordingly. The CFO should develop the financial forecasting tools to the point where the company's actual results closely resemble and merely confirm what the forecasting system accurately predicts.

- Take care not to overly engage in activities that while necessary, if overdone distract from the activities that add meaningful long term value to the organization. The CFO should focus his or her energy and time on working with the executive management team to build long-term, sustainable value for the organization and devote the vast majority of his or her time on those activities.

Pretty simple, huh?

Acknowledgements

Many thanks to Barbara Stewart, Accelus Partners LLC, for inspiring me to get this book over the finish line and to my publisher, Sequoia Di Angelo for having faith in this rookie.

Appendix

Exhibit: Cash Flow Forecasting Trend

	Week (- 13)	Week (- 12)	Weeks (- 11) to Week (- 3)	Week (- 2)	Week (- 1)	Current Week	Week (+ 1)	Weeks (+ 2) to Week (+25)	Week (+26)
Week (- 13)	321,651	320,986	-	308,534	312,246	8,301	311,663	-	
Week (- 12)		321,468	-	311,807	315,558	1,571	314,968	-	
Weeks (- 11 to Week - 3)									
Week (- 2)				312,151	314,235	0,250	313,646		
Week (- 1)					314,050	0,125	313,521	-	
Current Forecast						0,128	312,981	-	374,551

NOTE: A minus (-) week represents a cash flow week in the past. For example, if you look at the column labeled "Week (- 12)"; 12 weeks ago the actual cash on hand was $321,468, whereas the week before, the company had forecasted $320,986 of cash on hand. Conversely, with a (+) week. For example, if you look at the column labeled "Week (+1)", 14 weeks ago, the company had forecasted cash on hand of $311,663 (the forecast from Week (-13)), whereas in the current week's forecast, the company is now forecasting cash on hand of $312,981.

Biography

The Successful CFO

Anthony 'Tony' Tripodo is an accomplished executive with more than 35 years of experience in the energy industry leading companies at both the board and management level. Tony possesses extensive board level experience serving on audit, compensation, compliance and governance committees, as well as chairing audit and compliance committees. Tony's experience on both an executive and board level has involved companies with broad global reach for both publicly traded and private equity held companies. Tony currently serves as Executive Vice President and Senior Advisor as well as a member of the board of directors of Helix ESG, a leading offshore energy service company listed on the NYSE.

Tony's involvement at Helix began as an independent director in 2003 and in 2008 was asked by the board of directors to step into the Company as CFO with a mandate to work with the CEO to restructure the Company for sustainable future growth and with a solid financial foundation. Tony was reappointed to the board in 2015.

Tony has served as Chief Financial Officer of 3 publicly traded companies in the energy industry all of which possessed broad global reach requiring the CFO to deal with complex cross border transactions and hedging strategies. Tony's global perspective has been enhanced while serving on the board of directors of an Oslo, Norway and London, England based company.

Named by the Houston Business Journal as CFO of the Year in 2014 in recognition of his efforts in successfully navigating Helix through the financial and industry crisis of 2008. Tony serves as a Governing Body Chair of the Houston CFO Executive Summit.

Tony graduated Summa Cum Laude from St. Thomas University, and currently resides in Houston, Texas with his wife and 5 children.

CPSIA information can be obtained
at www.ICGtesting.com
Printed in the USA
BVOW07*2050051017
496714BV00002B/5/P